Real Gold or Digital Gold Investing

Roggie Clark

Learn Macro and Micro Economics, With This One Book

Whether you're a student, a professional, or simply someone eager to understand the world around you, this book is your perfect introduction to the fundamentals of micro and macroeconomics.

https://www.amazon.com/Macro-Micro-Economics-Made-Beginners-ebook/dp/B0DPHTFVQG

How to Sell Gold Jewelry for Cash and Avoid Scams

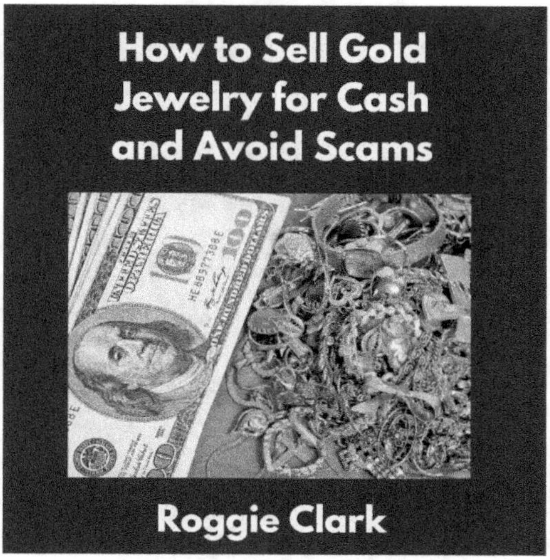

This book was written to help everyday people sell their gold with confidence, protect themselves from common tricks, and get the most money possible.

https://www.amazon.com/Sell-Gold-Jewelry-Avoid-Scams-ebook/dp/B0FW6R6TYN

Learn How To Invest in Gold Bars With This Book

Whether you're new to investing or seeking to diversify your portfolio, this beginner-friendly guide will give you the knowledge and confidence to invest in gold, and other precious metals.

https://www.amazon.com/Ultimate-Investing-Buying-Guide-Beginners-ebook/dp/B0F1KWWDXG

Learn How To Invest in Silver With This Book

The Ultimate Silver Investing & Buying Guide For Beginners is your clear, no-nonsense guide to incorporating silver into your wealth-building strategy.

https://www.amazon.com/Ultimate-Silver-Investing-Buying-Beginners-ebook

Get Out of Credit Card Debt With This Book

Are you tired of living paycheck to paycheck? Drowning in interest rates and minimum payments that never seem to shrink your balance? *Understanding & Overcoming Credit Card Debt* is your roadmap to financial freedom.

https://www.amazon.com/dp/B0F3WCVWG8

Copyright

Title: Real Gold or Digital Gold Investing
Author: Roggie Clark

Disclaimer

The views and opinions expressed in this book are those of the author and do not necessarily reflect the official policy or position of any individual, company, or organization cited or referenced in the text. The author is not affiliated with any of the individuals, companies, or organizations mentioned in the text, nor does the author receive any form of compensation for citing or referencing them.

The professional information in this text is distributed on an "as is" basis, without warranty. While every precaution has been taken in the preparation of the text, neither the author nor the publisher shall have any liability to any person or entity with respect to any loss or damage caused or alleged to be caused directly or indirectly by the instructions contained in this text or by the computer software and hardware products described in it.

The author nor the publisher does not guarantee any specific results or outcomes, and the information provided in this text should not be construed as professional advice. Readers should always consult with a qualified professional before making any significant changes to their website or business.

By reading this text, you agree that the author nor the publisher is responsible for any direct, indirect, incidental, or consequential damages that may arise from the use of the information provided. You assume full responsibility for any actions taken based on the information presented in this text.

Table of Contents

Introduction

I want to begin this book by addressing something you already know instinctively. The world of investing has changed faster in the last fifteen years than it did in the fifty years before it. As you look around, you see people treating digital assets as if they are just as real as physical metals, and you might be wondering how these two very different forms of value can even be compared.

I wrote this book to give you clarity, because I know how overwhelming it can feel when everyone online seems confident, loud, and contradictory at the same time. My goal is to help you understand the strengths and weaknesses of both real gold and digital gold from a grounded and practical perspective.

As you move through these chapters, I want you to feel equipped, not confused. You deserve information that respects your intelligence, guides your thinking, and gives you a clearer way to navigate this modern investment landscape.

Why Investors Compare Gold and Crypto

As you explore this topic, you will notice that investors tend to compare gold and crypto more than almost any other two assets. I believe this comparison happens because both are tied to the idea of protecting wealth, but they take completely different forms. When you look at physical gold, you see history, tradition, and a long record of holding value. When you look at digital gold, such as Bitcoin, you see innovation, technology, and a new way of defining what value even means.

These two worlds do not naturally fit together, yet investors continue to place them side by side because each attempts to solve the same problem. That problem is the fear of losing your purchasing power (currency devaluation) in a world where currencies shift, governments change policies, and markets behave unpredictably. Understanding this comparison is your first step toward seeing the bigger picture of why this book matters.

The Purpose of This Book

I wrote this book to help you feel confident enough to evaluate both real gold and digital gold on your own terms. Instead of relying on slogans, hype, or social media claims, you will learn how each asset actually works in the real world.

My purpose is not to convince you to choose one over the other but to help you understand what each one brings to the table. As you go deeper into the chapters, you will see that real gold and digital gold are not enemies competing for the same space. Rather, they are tools that can play different roles in your financial planning.

My goal is to offer clarity, balance, and practical explanations that remove the confusion surrounding these topics. By the end, you will see exactly how both forms of value can support your long term financial goals.

How to Use This Guide

I designed this guide to move step by step, and I encourage you to treat it like a learning journey rather than something you skim quickly. As you read, I want you to absorb the explanations, reflect on the comparisons, and consider how each concept relates to your own financial goals. You do not need any technical background before starting, because I will break down every concept in a clear and professional way.

The chapters are structured to build on each other so you always feel like your understanding is growing instead of jumping from topic to topic. If you already know some things about gold or crypto, you can use this guide to deepen that knowledge and correct any misconceptions you may have picked up. If you are brand new, this book will give you a strong and well balanced foundation that you can rely on as you continue to learn. When you finish, you will have a clear framework that helps you think like an informed and responsible investor.

Last Thoughts

As you begin this book, I want you to view it as a practical tool that connects modern digital innovation to the timeless role of real gold. Both forms of value exist in a world that is changing more rapidly than most investors realize, and you deserve to understand how these changes affect your financial decisions.

This introduction sets the tone for the deeper discussions that follow, giving you a starting point that is grounded, balanced, and easy to build upon. In the next chapters, you will move from basic definitions into real comparisons, and you will see how the pieces fit together. My hope is that each page strengthens your understanding and gives you more clarity than you had before you opened this book.

Chapter 1: The Basics of Real Gold

When you think about real gold, you are not just looking at a shiny metal. You are looking at something that has carried value across civilizations, cultures, and economic cycles for thousands of years. I want to start this chapter by helping you understand why gold is more than a collectible or a luxury item, because its story is directly connected to why people still rely on it today.

As you move through this chapter, you will see how gold earns its reputation as a stable and trusted store of value. My goal is to guide you through the basics in a way that feels clear, practical, and grounded in reality so you can build a strong understanding before comparing it to digital gold later.

By the time you finish this chapter, you will have a solid foundation that prepares you for the deeper discussions coming in the next sections of the book.

What Real Gold Is

When I talk about real gold, I am referring to the physical, tangible metal that you can hold in your hand. You might think of gold bars, coins, or jewelry, but in investing terms, we are usually focusing on **bullion** that has a specific purity and weight. Gold, in scientific terms, is a chemical element that does not corrode, tarnish, or decay, which is part of why it has retained value for so long. When you look at physical gold as an investment, you are dealing with something that is universally recognized and globally traded.

Unlike paper assets, it does not need a contract or digital system to prove its worth. You can carry it across borders, store it privately, and trade it almost anywhere in the world. This universality is one of the reasons investors still see gold as a foundational asset in times of economic uncertainty.

Why Gold Holds Value

If you have ever wondered why gold has held value for thousands of years, the answer is tied to both its physical qualities and its social history. Gold is rare but not too rare, and it takes real effort, time, and resources to mine it. This built in scarcity gives it a natural price floor that does not depend on a government or a financial institution.

Another key reason gold holds value is that people across cultures agree that it is valuable, which makes it a form of trust that has survived countless economic systems. When currencies fail or markets crash, gold often rises because people move toward assets that feel reliable and familiar. I want you to see gold as something that carries a long standing psychological and historical weight that reinforces its role in modern investing.

Types of Gold Investments

As you explore gold investing, you will notice there are several forms of gold available, each with its own benefits. The most common types are **physical bullion**, which includes bars and coins that you can store yourself. Many investors choose government minted coins because they are easy to trade and recognize, while others prefer bars because they often carry lower premiums.

You also have **collectible coins**, known as **numismatics**, but these have value tied to rarity and condition instead of gold content, which makes them less predictable. Some investors choose fractional pieces, which allow you to buy smaller amounts at a time. Each type of gold investment has pros and cons, and part of becoming a confident investor is understanding which option fits your financial goals and comfort level.

Physical Storage and Security

Once you own physical gold, you must think about how and where to store it. I want to prepare you for this step because many beginners underestimate how important secure storage really is. You can choose to keep your gold at home in a safe, store it in a bank safe deposit box, or use a private vaulting service. Each option has its advantages and limitations, and your choice depends on how much gold you have and how much control you want over it.

Storing gold at home gives you direct access, but it also requires proper security measures. Bank boxes offer protection but limit access during certain hours. Private vaults offer higher security but come with ongoing fees. This part of the process demonstrates that physical gold is not just an investment, but also a responsibility.

Costs, Premiums, and Liquidity

When you buy gold, you pay more than the market spot price. The extra cost above spot is called the **premium**, which includes dealer fees, manufacturing costs, and market demand. Bars usually have lower premiums than coins because they are cheaper to produce.

Liquidity refers to how quickly and easily you can sell your gold, and this varies based on what type you own. Coins from major mints are often the easiest to liquidate because they are widely recognized and trusted. Bars are also liquid but may require verification in some cases. Understanding these costs and liquidity factors helps you make smarter purchasing decisions and prevents you from being caught off guard when buying or selling.

Last Thoughts

As you close this chapter, I hope you are starting to appreciate the stability and clarity that real gold brings to the world of investing. You learned what gold is, why it holds value, how different forms of gold fit into an investment strategy, and what it takes to store and manage it responsibly.

These basics give you a strong foundation and a realistic understanding of what it means to own a physical asset. This chapter also prepared you for the comparisons you will encounter later when we introduce digital gold and explore how the two assets complement or oppose each other. With this foundation in place, you are ready to move into the next chapter where we break down the meaning and structure of digital gold.

Chapter 2: The Basics of Digital Gold

As you step into the world of digital gold, I want you to approach this topic with curiosity and an open mind. Digital assets can feel complex at first, especially if you come from a traditional investing background, but my goal in this chapter is to make everything feel clear and practical. When people talk about digital gold, they are usually referring to crypto assets that serve as a modern store of value, with Bitcoin being the most well known example.

You might hear about these assets in the news, on social media, or from friends, but the information is often filled with hype or confusion. I want to remove those layers so you can understand what digital gold actually is and why it has gained such a strong place in modern finance. By the time you finish this chapter, you will have a more confident grasp of what makes digital gold unique, how it functions, and why so many investors are paying attention to it.

What Digital Gold Means

When I use the phrase digital gold, I am talking about a digital asset that aims to mimic the store of value qualities that physical gold has held for thousands of years. Bitcoin is the most direct example because its supply is limited, its issuance schedule is predictable, and it is decentralized. This means no single government or organization controls it, which is part of what makes people compare it to gold.

Instead of holding something in your hand, you hold a digital record that proves ownership of a specific amount of the asset. Because it exists on a public and decentralized system, its value is determined by market demand rather than a central authority. For many investors, digital gold represents a bridge between traditional investing and modern technology, and that combination has made it an increasingly popular choice.

Intro to Blockchain and Bitcoin

To understand digital gold, you need to understand blockchain technology, because it is the foundation that makes everything possible. A blockchain is a public, secure, and decentralized ledger that records every transaction made with a digital asset.

Instead of trusting a bank or institution to verify transactions, the blockchain uses a network of computers that follow strict rules to confirm and record each action. Bitcoin, the most well known digital gold asset, operates on this system and uses a process called mining to add new blocks to the chain.

This creates transparency, security, and immutability, meaning once something is recorded on the blockchain, it cannot be changed. I want you to see blockchain as the technical backbone that gives digital gold its strength, reliability, and global accessibility. With this understanding, you can better grasp why digital gold is designed to be resistant to manipulation and control.

Why Crypto Is Viewed as a Store of Value

When investors talk about digital assets as a store of value, they are usually referring to specific features that mirror the strengths of real gold. Bitcoin, for example, has a capped supply of twenty one million units, which creates scarcity similar to mined metals.

This is a major reason people view it as a hedge against inflation and currency devaluation. Another reason is decentralization. Because it is not controlled by a government or central bank, it is less vulnerable to political decisions that can weaken traditional currencies.

Many investors also see the portability of digital gold as a benefit, because you can transfer it globally within minutes without physical transportation. These characteristics have shaped a growing belief that digital gold can hold value in both stable and unstable economies.

Types of Crypto Assets

When you enter the digital asset space, you will quickly notice that there are many types of crypto assets available. Not all of them qualify as digital gold, and I want to make sure you can tell the difference. Bitcoin is the primary digital gold asset because of its structure and purpose. Ethereum and other altcoins serve different functions, such as powering decentralized applications or smart contracts.

There are also stablecoins, which are tied to the value of traditional currencies, but these do not act as a store of value like gold. Some assets have utility features, while others focus on innovation or experimentation. As you explore these options, keep in mind that digital gold is a specific category, not a general label. Understanding these differences helps you stay focused on assets that are designed to store value rather than take on unnecessary risk.

Wallets, Exchanges, and Security Basics

Once you decide to enter the digital gold space, you need to understand how wallets and exchanges work. A digital wallet is a tool that stores your private keys, which prove ownership of your digital assets. Exchanges are platforms where you can buy, sell, and trade crypto, but you do not truly control your assets on an exchange unless you move them into your own wallet.

This concept is often summed up in the phrase not your keys, not your coins. Private wallets come in different forms, such as hardware wallets, mobile wallets, and desktop wallets, each with different levels of security. As you explore these tools, you should prioritize security first, because the digital world requires careful management of your information and access. Taking the time to understand wallets and exchanges helps protect your digital gold from theft, hacks, or accidental loss.

Last Thoughts

As you finish this chapter, I want you to feel confident about what digital gold really represents and how it fits into the broader world of investing. You learned what digital gold means, how blockchain technology supports it, why certain assets act as stores of value, and what tools you need to handle them safely. This knowledge gives you a strong foundation that pairs with what you learned in the previous chapter about physical gold.

When you compare these two forms of value later in the book, you will be able to see the similarities and differences with a clearer and more informed perspective. With this understanding in place, you are ready to move into the next chapter, where we begin a direct comparison between real gold and digital gold.

Chapter 3: Gold vs Crypto, A Direct Comparison

Now that you understand the foundations of both real gold and digital gold, this chapter brings them face to face so you can see how they truly compare. I want you to approach this section with a practical mindset and understand how each asset performs differently under various conditions. When you look at gold and crypto side by side, you begin to see how investor behavior, technology, accessibility, and market structure shape their strengths and weaknesses.

My aim in this chapter is to help you build a clear mental map so that you can place each asset in its proper role within the modern financial landscape. By the end of this chapter, you will see why investors continue to debate them and why it can be important to understand both.

Volatility and Stability

One of the first comparisons investors look at is volatility, because it affects how confidently you can hold an asset during market swings. Gold is known for stability, and it has built this reputation over centuries of economic cycles. It tends to move slowly, rising in uncertain times and leveling off as markets stabilize.

Crypto, on the other hand, often experiences dramatic price swings in short periods of time. These rapid movements can create opportunities (i.e. buying the "dip"), but they can also introduce significant emotional and financial stress. You might find that crypto offers higher reward potential, but it also carries higher risk, in other words, it's no different than gambling.

While on the other hand, gold provides consistency and acts as an anchor in an otherwise unpredictable market. Understanding this difference helps you balance your expectations and your risk tolerance.

Liquidity and Access

Liquidity is another critical factor when comparing these two assets. Gold is widely accepted and easy to sell, especially if you own coins or bars from recognized mints. You can sell gold to dealers, private buyers, or trading platforms with minimal friction.

Crypto, however, offers a different type of liquidity. It allows you to trade globally, twenty four hours a day, without waiting for business hours or geographic limitations. This level of access can be appealing, but it also depends on your ability to use secure exchanges and understand digital tools. While gold requires physical handling, crypto requires technical knowledge.

Inflation Protection

When it comes to inflation protection, gold has known benefits while digital gold offers potential benefits as well. Gold has a long history of rising during periods of currency weakness because it carries intrinsic value that does not depend on government policies. Investors often use it as a **safe haven asset** when they fear the purchasing power of their currency is declining.

Crypto, particularly Bitcoin, offers inflation protection through its fixed supply. Because no one can create more than the set limit, many investors view it as a shield against monetary expansion. The challenge with crypto is that its short history means we have less long term data to evaluate. Also, crypto is becoming more regulated, while gold doesn't have universal regulation. So essentially, gold is the tested option, while digital gold is the emerging alternative. Seeing them through this lens allows you to understand why both attract investors concerned about inflation.

Supply Limits and Scarcity

Scarcity is one of the most important qualities of store of value assets, and both gold and digital gold express this quality in unique ways. Gold is scarce because it takes real resources, time, and physical effort to mine and refine it. Even with modern mining technology, it remains difficult to access, which helps maintain its value.

Bitcoin also has built in scarcity, but it is controlled through code rather than physical extraction. There will never be more than twenty one million Bitcoins, and this cap creates a predictable and transparent supply schedule. The difference is that gold scarcity is natural, while digital scarcity is engineered.

Understanding these two types of scarcity helps you appreciate how each asset attempts to protect long term value.

Real World Use Cases

When comparing these assets, it is important to look at how they function in the real world. Gold has industrial uses in electronics, dentistry, and manufacturing, which support its demand beyond investing. It is also used for jewelry, cultural ceremonies, and central bank reserves. These practical uses reinforce its value.

Digital gold does not have physical applications, but it plays a growing role in modern financial systems. People use it for cross border transfers, digital payments, and as a hedge against unstable banking environments. Some investors also use crypto to diversify away from traditional financial institutions. Each asset has distinct real world roles, and understanding these roles helps you see how they fit into a balanced strategy.

Last Thoughts

This chapter brings together the similarities and differences that define real gold and digital gold, giving you a clear view of how each asset performs in key areas. You explored volatility, liquidity, inflation protection, scarcity, and real world use cases, and you now have a stronger sense of where each asset shines.

This comparison prepares you for the deeper analysis in the next chapter, where we examine how both gold and digital gold behave during economic stress. As you continue forward, you will notice how the concepts from this chapter build directly into the next set of insights. With this context in place, you are ready to explore how these assets react when markets become uncertain and investor behavior shifts. Also, I hope you can tell that gold is more secure, and a long-standing asset, while crypto, brings much more volatility, and possible worry.

Chapter 4: How Each Asset Performs During Economic Stress

When you evaluate any asset, one of the most revealing tests is how it behaves during periods of economic stress. I want you to look at this chapter as a deeper look into investor psychology, market behavior, and the real world conditions that influence both real gold and digital gold. It is easy to feel confident about an asset when the economy is stable, but the true measure of its strength comes during recessions, market crashes, or times of uncertainty.

As you read through these sections, I want you to notice the patterns that appear repeatedly and how they influence investor decisions. My goal is to help you understand how each type of asset reacts under pressure so you can see how they fit into a resilient financial strategy. By the time you finish this chapter, you will have a clearer picture of how gold and crypto behave when the stakes are highest.

Gold in Recessions

Gold has a long track record of performing well during recessions because investors trust it as a stable and reliable store of value. When the economy weakens, people often move away from stocks or riskier assets and shift toward gold as a protective measure. This pattern is not new.

You can find examples of gold rising during recessions across many periods of history because it does not depend on corporate profits or government decisions to hold its worth. Central banks also tend to increase their gold holdings during uncertain times, which reinforces demand.

As an investor, you can take comfort in knowing that gold is supported by centuries of market behavior. It is not perfect, and it does not always rise instantly, but it has proven itself repeatedly as a safe option during economic downturns.

Crypto in Recessions

Crypto behaves differently during recessions because it is still a relatively new asset class with a shorter market history. In many cases, crypto has shown high volatility when the economy weakens, which can be challenging if you are not prepared for rapid price swings.

Investors often debate whether digital gold will eventually behave more like traditional safe haven assets, but right now the data shows that crypto tends to react more like a high risk investment like stocks, futures, derivatives, annuities, etc.). During uncertain periods, many investors pull back from speculative assets, and this pressure can push crypto prices downward.

However, there are also unique moments when crypto has performed well during localized crises. In regions with unstable currencies or limited banking access, digital gold has sometimes served as a protective outlet. This shows that crypto has potential as a hedge, but it is not yet consistent enough to rely on during every recession.

Market Crashes and Corrections

During market crashes, you can learn a great deal about an asset's true behavior. Gold typically performs well during these events because investors view it as a stable alternative when stocks are falling. In some cases, gold rises sharply as people rush to buy safe assets. There are also moments when gold dips briefly during the very beginning of a crash because investors liquidate everything to raise cash, but it often stabilizes later.

Crypto, on the other hand, usually reacts immediately and dramatically during major market downturns. Prices can fall rapidly as traders try to exit their positions, leading to sharp declines. Even though crypto has experienced recovery after crashes, the initial reaction is often unpredictable. Understanding these differences helps you see where each asset stands in terms of risk and stability during extreme market events.

Historical Patterns

Gold has centuries of historical patterns that show how it performs in different economic conditions. You can look back through wars, currency collapses, inflation cycles, and market crashes and find consistent evidence that gold holds value over time. This long history gives you a reliable guide for future expectations.

Crypto, in contrast, is only a little over a decade old, which means we have less historical data to work with. The patterns that do exist show strong growth during bull markets and high volatility during corrections. Without a long record, it is harder to predict how crypto will behave in rare or severe economic events.

As an investor, recognizing the difference between long term historical certainty and short term emerging patterns is essential. It helps you understand why some people trust gold deeply while others invest in crypto for its potential rather than its proven reliability.

Behavior of Investors Under Stress

One of the most revealing ways to compare these assets is by observing how investors behave under stress. When fear increases, many investors fall back on familiar assets, and gold benefits from this instinct. People trust what they understand, and gold's long history makes it emotionally comfortable to hold during uncertain times. Crypto attracts a different type of mindset.

Some investors see crashes as opportunities to buy more digital assets at lower prices, while others panic due to the rapid volatility. This split in behavior shows that crypto still has a psychological barrier to overcome before it can be viewed as a true safe haven.

As you consider your own reactions, it is helpful to understand how your personal risk tolerance plays into these decisions. Knowing how investors as a whole behave under pressure gives you insight into how each asset might perform in a crisis.

Last Thoughts

This chapter helps you see how gold and digital gold behave when markets become unstable, and this insight is essential as you build your understanding of both assets. You explored recessions, market crashes, historical patterns, and investor behavior, all of which show clear differences in stability and predictability.

Gold remains the trusted option during stress, while digital gold offers potential but still shows inconsistent reactions in difficult times. This deeper understanding connects directly to the next chapter, where we examine the risks that come with owning each type of asset.

By carrying this knowledge forward, you will be better prepared to evaluate which risks matter most to you and how they influence your investment decisions.

Chapter 5: Risk Factors You Must Understand

Every investment comes with risks, and understanding those risks is one of the most important steps you can take as a responsible investor. In this chapter, I want to guide you through the unique challenges that come with both real gold and digital gold so you can make decisions with confidence rather than uncertainty.

Many people focus only on the rewards of an asset, but overlooking the risks can lead to stress, losses, or disappointment. As you move through these sections, I want you to think about how each risk affects your long term financial goals.

My goal is to give you a clear and balanced look at what could go wrong, why it happens, and how you can prepare yourself. By the end of this chapter, you will understand the realities behind both types of assets rather than relying on assumptions or hype.

Gold Risks

When you invest in real gold, the risks are different from those of most financial assets, but they are still important to consider. One of the biggest risks is storage because you must keep your gold physically safe, which can introduce costs or vulnerabilities. If you store gold at home, you face risks such as theft or property damage.

If you use a vault, you face ongoing fees and limited access during emergencies. Another risk is that gold prices do not always rise quickly. Gold can remain flat for long periods, which can be frustrating if you are expecting rapid growth. There is also the risk of counterfeit gold, especially when buying from sellers who do not verify authenticity. Understanding these risks helps you approach gold with realistic expectations and better planning.

Crypto Risks

Crypto assets come with their own set of risks, many of which are tied to the digital nature of the investment. One major risk is extreme price volatility, which can create significant gains but also steep losses. If you are new to crypto, the rapid price swings can be emotionally challenging and may push you to make rushed decisions.

Another risk is security because crypto stored on exchanges is vulnerable to hacks or platform failures. If you lose your private keys, you lose access to your assets permanently, which makes self custody both powerful and risky. You also face the risk of scams, rug pulls, and fraudulent projects in the broader crypto space. These risks remind you that digital gold requires careful management, research, and a willingness to learn the technology behind it.

Security Threats

Security threats affect both gold and crypto, but in very different ways. With gold, physical theft is the most obvious threat, especially if your storage setup is not secure. You must think about safes, alarm systems, and insurance. Crypto security threats revolve around digital vulnerabilities. Hackers target exchanges, wallets, and personal devices, and a single mistake can lead to irreversible losses.

Phishing attacks, malware, and fake applications are common risks for crypto holders. Unlike physical theft, digital theft can happen silently and instantly. Understanding these different types of threats helps you build a secure environment for your assets, whether they are stored in a vault or on a hardware wallet.

Market Manipulation

Both gold and crypto markets can be influenced by large players, and this introduces another layer of risk. In the gold market, large institutional investors and central banks can move prices through big purchases or sales. Paper gold markets, such as futures, can also affect pricing even when no physical gold changes hands.

Crypto markets face different forms of manipulation. Whales, or large holders, can influence prices by buying or selling in large volumes. Some crypto projects are built with unfair token distribution, which allows insiders to manipulate markets behind the scenes.

Social media hype can also create artificial price movements. As an investor, recognizing these dynamics helps you stay grounded and avoid decisions based on noise or sudden market swings.

Regulation and Policy Changes

Regulatory risks are important because governments around the world treat gold and crypto very differently. Gold has a long history of global acceptance, but it is still subject to policies around taxes, imports, and reporting requirements. In rare historical cases, governments have even restricted ownership, which shows that policy changes can influence gold markets.

Crypto faces much more regulatory uncertainty because it is a newer asset class. Governments continue to debate how to classify, tax, or restrict digital assets. Regulations can affect exchanges, stablecoins, mining operations, and even individual investors. Sudden policy changes can cause rapid market reactions, and understanding this uncertainty helps you stay prepared for possible shifts.

Last Thoughts

This chapter highlights the risks that come with both real gold and digital gold, giving you a clearer view of the challenges you may face as an investor. You learned about storage issues, volatility, security threats, market manipulation, and government policy, all of which play major roles in how these assets behave. By recognizing these risks upfront, you put yourself in a stronger position to make thoughtful and informed investment decisions.

This understanding connects directly to the next chapter, where we explore how to build a balanced and strategic approach that aligns with your goals. With this knowledge in hand, you are ready to move forward and learn how to construct a smarter and more resilient investment plan.

Chapter 6: Building a Balanced Investment Approach

As you move deeper into this topic, I want to shift your focus from understanding each asset to understanding how they can work together within your overall financial strategy. Building a balanced investment approach is not about choosing sides, but about learning how different assets support your long term goals.

In this chapter, I want to help you think like a planner rather than a collector. Gold offers stability, while digital gold offers innovation and growth potential, and your task is to decide how much of each you want in your portfolio.

A balanced approach reduces stress, protects you during uncertain times, and gives you more control over your financial future. By the time you finish this chapter, you will know how to evaluate your needs, measure your risk tolerance, and build a straightforward plan that you can adjust as your situation evolves.

Diversification Basics

Diversification is one of the most important principles in investing because it helps you reduce risk while still allowing for growth. When you spread your money across different types of assets, you protect yourself from relying too heavily on one investment.

Gold and crypto can both play valuable roles in a diversified portfolio because they behave differently during various market conditions. Gold tends to hold value during downturns, while crypto may offer strong growth during bull markets. By combining them, you create a more balanced and adaptable strategy, but personally, I lean towards real gold, and generally avoid crypto, but that's just me.

Diversification is not just about owning many assets. It is about choosing assets that complement each other so your overall portfolio remains stable even when individual parts fluctuate.

Short Term vs Long Term Strategy

Your strategy changes depending on whether you are investing for the short term or the long term. If you are thinking short term, you need to be ready for volatility because crypto can experience sudden movements. Short term investing usually requires more active monitoring and quicker decision making.

Long term investing, on the other hand, allows you to ride out market fluctuations and focus on the bigger picture. Gold works well as a long term store of value because it has a consistent record of stability.

Digital gold could be a powerful long term asset, if you believe in its adoption and technological foundations. When you understand your timeline, you can choose a strategy that fits your lifestyle and helps you stay committed through market changes.

Understanding Your Risk Tolerance

One of the most personal parts of building a balanced investment approach is understanding your risk tolerance. Your risk tolerance reflects how much uncertainty you can handle without feeling overwhelmed. Everyone is different, and there is no right or wrong amount of risk.

I want you to think honestly about how you react to market swings. Do you feel anxious when prices drop, or are you comfortable waiting through volatility? Gold appeals to investors who prefer stability, while digital gold appeals to those who can handle uncertainty.

Knowing your limits helps you build a portfolio that brings confidence rather than stress. When you align your investments with your natural comfort level, you make better decisions and stay consistent over time.

Creating a Simple Portfolio Plan

A simple portfolio plan can help you stay organized and focused as you build your investment strategy. Start by deciding what percentage of your portfolio you want to allocate to gold and digital gold. You might choose a structure like 90 percent gold and 10 percent digital gold if you value stability. This is not investment advice. After setting your percentages, choose the specific types of gold and digital assets you want to hold.

Decide whether you will buy physical coins or bars, or whether you will use a hardware wallet for your crypto. A good plan also includes a schedule for reviewing your portfolio, adjusting allocations, and tracking your progress. Keeping your plan simple ensures that you stay consistent without feeling overwhelmed.

Last Thoughts

This chapter gives you the tools to build a balanced, thoughtful, and personalized investment approach that blends both real gold and digital gold. You explored diversification, asset mixing, short and long term strategies, risk tolerance, and simple portfolio planning.

These insights help you build a stable foundation for your financial future while giving you the flexibility to grow with changing markets.

As you move into the next chapter, you will explore the cost factors behind each asset, which will help you refine your strategy even further. With this understanding, you are ready to examine the true financial realities behind buying, holding, and selling both gold and digital gold.

Chapter 7: The Cost Factor

When you compare real gold and digital gold, one of the most practical and sometimes overlooked considerations is the true cost of owning each asset. Costs affect your investment results more than you may realize, and understanding them helps you avoid unpleasant surprises in the future. In this chapter, I want to walk you through the full range of expenses you may encounter when buying, holding, and selling both assets so you can build a strategy that matches your financial goals.

These costs can influence your returns, your access, and even your long term confidence in your investment choices. As you move through these sections, I want you to think about how each type of cost fits your lifestyle and your comfort level. By the end of this chapter, you will know how to measure the real value of an investment by looking beyond the price tag.

Buying Costs

When you buy real gold, you pay more than the spot price because dealers charge a premium that covers manufacturing, shipping, and business overhead. Coins often have higher premiums than bars because they are easier to trade and come from recognized mints. If you buy from a trusted dealer, you pay for reliability and authenticity, which reduces your risk of receiving counterfeit products. In contrast, buying digital gold usually involves exchange fees, spread costs, and sometimes network fees.

These costs can vary based on the platform you use and the type of asset you purchase. A thought about digital gold is that you can buy small amounts without significant overhead, which makes it accessible for beginners. Understanding these differences helps you decide which buying structure fits your budget and your long term plans.

Selling Costs

Selling real gold also comes with costs that you should prepare for. Dealers buy gold below spot price to protect their own margins, which means you may receive less than you expect when selling. If you are selling coins, the buyback price may be higher than for bars, but this depends on market demand. In some cases, you may also pay authentication or refining fees for large amounts of gold.

Digital gold offers a different experience. When you sell crypto assets, you typically pay trading fees, and depending on the platform, you may also face withdrawal fees. Price slippage can occur if you sell a large amount quickly on a low liquidity exchange. Knowing how these costs work helps you plan your selling strategy and avoid unnecessary losses.

Fees and Hidden Expenses

Beyond basic buying and selling costs, there are hidden expenses that many investors overlook. For gold, storage costs can add up over time if you use a private vault or bank deposit box. Insurance may also be necessary if you keep gold at home or in a vault. Transportation costs can appear when moving gold between locations.

For digital gold, hidden expenses often appear in the form of network transaction fees, subscription fees for certain platforms, or higher spreads during periods of extreme volatility. Some investors also face security costs if they use premium hardware wallets or safeguarding services.

These hidden expenses show that the true cost of ownership depends on more than just initial prices. When you account for them, you gain a more accurate understanding of your investment.

Storage vs Digital Security

One of the clearest distinctions between real gold and digital gold is how you protect each asset after purchase. Physical gold requires secure storage, whether in a home safe, a vault, or a bank. This introduces ongoing responsibilities, such as maintenance, insurance, and accessibility planning.

Digital gold shifts the responsibility toward digital security, where you must protect your private keys, devices, and accounts. You may need hardware wallets, backup systems, or cybersecurity habits to keep your digital assets safe. While physical gold requires physical effort, digital gold requires technical discipline.

Understanding your comfort level with both forms of responsibility helps you choose the path that feels manageable for your lifestyle.

Understanding True Ownership Costs

When you evaluate investments, you must look at the complete picture, not just the purchase price. True ownership cost includes the time, effort, fees, and responsibilities that come with managing an asset. Gold demands physical care, storage planning, and insurance, while digital gold demands cybersecurity awareness and careful handling of your private information. You should also consider opportunity costs. For example, if you invest heavily in one asset, you may limit your ability to explore others with better growth potential.

Understanding these broader costs helps you plan realistically and avoid taking on more commitment than you can comfortably manage. When you know what ownership truly requires, you make better decisions and set clear expectations for yourself.

Last Thoughts

This chapter gives you a detailed look at the real cost of owning both real gold and digital gold, which is essential for creating a solid and sustainable investment plan. You examined buying costs, selling costs, hidden fees, storage needs, and the deeper responsibilities that come with ownership. These insights help you see that cost is not just a number.

It is a combination of your time, your security efforts, and your long term financial commitment. As you move into the next chapter, you will explore the common myths and misunderstandings that can influence how people think about gold and crypto. With this knowledge, you are ready to approach those myths with a clearer and more informed perspective.

Chapter 8: Common Myths and Misunderstandings

As you learn more about real gold and digital gold, you will quickly discover that both assets are surrounded by myths, assumptions, and exaggerated claims. These beliefs can influence your decisions without you even realizing it, which is why this chapter is dedicated to separating fact from fiction. I want to help you approach each asset with clarity and accuracy so you do not rely on popular narratives that may mislead you.

My goal in this chapter is to explain where these myths come from, why they continue to spread, and how they can shape your expectations in harmful ways. When you understand the truth behind these misunderstandings, you build a more stable foundation for your investment decisions. By the time you finish this chapter, you will feel more confident identifying false claims and focusing on real data instead of hype.

Myths About Gold

There are several myths about gold that can confuse new investors, and one of the most common is the belief that gold always rises during every economic crisis. While gold often performs well in uncertain times, it can also remain flat or even decline before recovering.

Another myth is that gold is impossible to counterfeit. In reality, counterfeit gold exists, especially when buying from unverified sellers or private individuals. Some people also believe that gold is too expensive for beginners, but fractional pieces make it accessible for almost any budget.

There is also a belief that gold requires no maintenance or responsibility, but as you learned earlier, storage and insurance are real concerns. By understanding these myths, you approach gold with realistic expectations and avoid misleading claims.

Myths About Crypto

Crypto myths are widespread, partly because digital gold is still new and evolving. One common myth is that crypto is anonymous, but most blockchain transactions are traceable and publicly recorded. Another myth is that crypto is guaranteed to become the future of money, which is an assumption rather than a proven fact.

There is also a myth that crypto will always go up in value, but like any asset, it can experience long downturns. Many beginners also believe that crypto cannot be hacked, but exchanges, wallets, and personal devices remain targets for cybercriminals.

Breaking down these myths helps you see crypto for what it truly is instead of what online communities claim it to be.

Media Narratives

Media narratives play a large role in shaping public opinion about gold and digital gold. News outlets often exaggerate market swings, presenting gold as a panic asset or crypto as a get rich quick opportunity.

These narratives can create fear or excitement, leading people to make rushed decisions. Social media adds another layer of distortion because viral content often focuses on extreme events rather than realistic expectations. Sometimes influencers promote assets they do not fully understand or have financial incentives to exaggerate.

When you consume information from the media, it is important to recognize the difference between entertainment and meaningful analysis. Understanding media influence helps you maintain focus and make decisions based on research rather than emotion.

Marketing Hype

Marketing hype can strongly affect how people view both gold and crypto. Companies that sell gold may highlight only the benefits without acknowledging the responsibilities or costs of ownership. Crypto projects often use flashy language, promises of high returns, or the excitement of new technology to attract attention.

This hype can make you feel like you need to act quickly, even when it is better to take your time. In the world of crypto, hype can even drive entire market cycles, pushing prices up rapidly before they fall. Gold marketing can also oversimplify the asset, presenting it as a guaranteed safety net rather than a tool that requires careful planning. Recognizing hype allows you to slow down and examine the facts before making decisions.

What Beginners Often Get Wrong

Beginners in both gold and crypto often make similar mistakes that stem from misunderstandings about how these assets truly work. Many people invest without researching fees, risks, or storage requirements, which leads to frustration later. Others buy based on emotion instead of strategy, especially when prices are rising or falling sharply.

Some beginners assume that owning a single asset is enough to protect their financial future, but this approach ignores the importance of diversification. Many also fail to consider how long they plan to hold an asset or what role it should play in their broader financial goals.

These common mistakes can be avoided by learning the basics and approaching each asset with patience and discipline. When you understand what beginners often get wrong, you can make smarter decisions from the start.

Last Thoughts

This chapter helps you clear away the myths, assumptions, and exaggerated claims that often surround real gold and digital gold. You explored misunderstandings about both assets, the influence of media narratives, the power of marketing hype, and the common mistakes beginners make.

By cutting through the noise, you build a clearer and more realistic understanding of how these assets function. This perspective prepares you for the next chapter, where we focus on the future of gold and crypto and how long term trends may influence their value. With this clarity in place, you can move forward with stronger judgment and a more confident mindset.

Chapter 9: Real Gold or Digital Gold for the Future

As you look toward the future of investing, it is natural to wonder which asset will play the larger role in the years ahead. Gold has thousands of years of history behind it, while digital gold represents a technological shift that is still unfolding. In this chapter, I want to help you explore the long term possibilities of both assets so you can understand how they may evolve and what that means for you as an investor.

Instead of predicting one clear winner, I want to focus on the trends, behaviors, and innovations that will shape the market. My goal is to help you think through the future with a clear and balanced perspective, so you can make decisions that support your long term financial goals. By the time you reach the end of this chapter, you will have a deeper understanding of where real gold and digital gold may be heading.

Trends You Should Watch

Several important trends will influence the future of gold and digital gold in the coming decades. One of the major trends for gold is the increasing interest from central banks, many of which are buying gold at record levels. This suggests that gold will continue to play a role in global financial stability. For digital gold, trends such as blockchain adoption, institutional investment, and technological improvement are shaping its long term potential.

More countries and companies are exploring digital currencies, which expands familiarity with crypto based systems. Another trend to watch is the movement toward decentralized finance, where digital assets can serve new purposes beyond storing value. Paying attention to these trends helps you better anticipate how each asset may change over time.

Generational Investing Differences

Different generations approach investing in unique ways, and these differences will influence the future of gold and digital gold. Older generations often prefer real gold because it feels secure, familiar, and tied to long term stability. Younger generations, especially millennials and Gen Z, tend to be more open to digital assets because they grew up with technology and are comfortable with digital financial tools.

These generational differences will shape market demand in the years ahead. As younger investors gain more financial influence, digital gold may become a larger part of mainstream portfolios. At the same time, gold will likely remain valuable because it appeals to investors who prioritize safety and long term preservation. Understanding these generational patterns gives you insight into future market movements.

Technology and Currency Innovation

Technology plays a major role in shaping the future of digital gold. Blockchain innovations, faster networks, and improvements in security all influence how widely digital assets are adopted. Some countries are developing digital currencies, while others are exploring ways to integrate blockchain technology into financial systems. These innovations create pathways for digital gold to become more accessible and more widely used.

Gold, while not dependent on technology, is also influenced by innovation. New mining techniques, more efficient refining processes, and improved verification tools continue to support its value and global acceptance. Both assets benefit from technological change, but in very different ways. When you understand how technology shapes each asset, you gain a clearer view of their long term potential.

The Future of Store of Value Assets

As you consider the future of store of value assets, it is important to recognize that economic uncertainty will always influence investor behavior. Gold will likely continue to serve as a safe haven because it offers stability and physical security. It has survived every economic system humanity has created so far, which makes it uniquely trustworthy.

Digital gold offers a different kind of future. Its global accessibility, limited supply, and technological foundation position it as a potential long term store of value for a digital world. The future may involve a blend of both assets, where investors rely on gold for preservation and crypto for growth and global utility. Thinking about these possibilities helps you prepare for various long term scenarios.

Long Term Market Outlook

Long term outlooks for gold and digital gold depend on economic trends, technology adoption, and global investor behavior. Gold is expected to remain stable because it has a reliable historical performance that continues to attract conservative investors and central banks.

Its limited supply and global recognition support long term value. Digital gold, especially Bitcoin, has a more uncertain but potentially more dynamic future. If adoption increases and regulations evolve, digital gold could become a standard part of global portfolios.

However, if technological or regulatory barriers remain, its growth may slow. When you weigh these possibilities, you gain a better understanding of how each asset may fit into your own future strategy.

Last Thoughts

This chapter helps you explore the future potential of both real gold and digital gold, giving you a forward looking perspective that connects deeply with everything you have learned so far. You examined trends, generational differences, technological innovation, and long term market behavior. These insights help you understand that the future is not about choosing one asset over the other, but about recognizing the strengths each brings to a changing financial world.

As you move into the next chapter, you will have the opportunity to see how these ideas shape common questions that new investors often ask. With this future oriented foundation, you are ready to explore the practical answers that tie the entire book together.

Chapter 10: Frequently Asked Questions

As you reach this stage of the book, you may find yourself holding onto specific questions that did not fit neatly into earlier chapters. That is completely normal, and this chapter is designed to help you address the most common questions people ask when learning about real gold and digital gold. I want you to see this section as a practical guide that ties together what you have already learned and clears up any lingering uncertainties.

These questions reflect real concerns from new and experienced investors alike, and answering them helps you strengthen your understanding. Hopefully, by reading this, you will feel more prepared to make smart decisions, avoid common mistakes, and apply these insights to your own financial plans.

Beginner Questions

Beginners often want to know which asset is better to start with, and the truth is that the answer depends on your comfort level and goals. If you prefer stability and a slower pace, gold may feel like the easier starting point. If you are comfortable learning new technology and can handle price swings, digital gold might appeal more to you. Another common beginner question is how much money you need to start investing.

Gold and crypto are both accessible because you can buy small amounts, such as fractional gold pieces or small amounts of Bitcoin. Beginners also ask whether they need to hold both assets. While it is not required, owning a mix of gold and digital gold can give you a more balanced start. These simple questions help you see that the first steps are easier than they seem. Personally, for beginners, I recommend just starting out with physical assets like gold.

Practical Questions

Practical questions often revolve around storage, fees, and how to buy or sell each asset. Many people want to know whether it is safer to store gold at home or in a vault. The answer depends on your security setup and how much gold you own. For digital gold, people ask whether they should leave their crypto on an exchange or move it to a private wallet.

Self custody gives you more control but requires you to manage your own security. Others want to know when the best time is to buy or sell. Timing the market is difficult, but long term strategies help reduce pressure and improve results. Addressing these practical questions helps you gain confidence in managing both assets responsibly.

Safety and Security

Safety and security questions are some of the most important, especially for new investors. People often ask whether gold can be stolen easily and how to protect it. Using safes, alarms, and secure storage helps reduce risk. For digital gold, people want to know how to avoid hacks or phishing attacks. The most important steps include protecting your private keys, using hardware wallets, and avoiding suspicious links or offers.

Another security question involves whether digital gold can vanish or be erased. Blockchain technology can ensure that your holdings remain recorded as long as you protect your access. Understanding these security basics helps you safeguard your assets from common threats.

Market Behavior

New investors often wonder why gold and digital gold behave differently during market swings. Gold tends to move gradually and often rises during uncertainty because people trust it as a safe asset. Digital gold, on the other hand, reacts quickly and can experience sharp gains or losses in short periods. People also ask whether gold and crypto move in opposite directions.

While they sometimes behave differently, their relationship is not fixed and can change based on market conditions. Another common question is how global events affect these assets. Economic instability often pushes demand for gold, while technological or regulatory news often influences crypto. Knowing how market behavior shapes each asset helps you interpret price movements with more confidence.

Buying and Selling Basics

Many investors want to know the simplest way to buy or sell gold and digital gold. For gold, buying from reputable dealers or established platforms is usually the safest approach. You can choose coins or bars depending on your budget and storage plan. Selling gold requires awareness of premiums and buyback prices. For digital gold, buying through major exchanges is the easiest method.

You can sell your crypto on the same platforms, but you should be aware of trading fees and price slippage. Some investors also want to know whether buying small amounts over time is effective. Dollar cost averaging works well for both assets because it reduces emotional decision making. Learning these basics helps you build a confident buying and selling routine.

Last Thoughts

This chapter ties together many of the practical and emotional questions that often arise as people learn about real gold and digital gold. You explored beginner concerns, practical steps, safety measures, market behavior, and basic buying and selling strategies. These answers help you feel more grounded and supported as you move through your investment journey.

With these clarifications in place, you are ready to transition into the final chapter, where you will bring together everything you have learned and explore the core lessons you should carry forward. This final step will help you reflect on your progress and prepare for the decisions that lie ahead.

Conclusion

As you reach the end of this book, I want to take a moment to reflect on the journey you have taken. You explored both real gold and digital gold from their foundations all the way to their long term potential, and you gained insight into how these assets fit within the broader world of investing. My goal was to give you clarity, confidence, and a practical understanding that empowers you to make smart decisions.

As you have seen, real gold and digital gold each carry unique strengths, risks, and responsibilities, and understanding both gives you a wider range of tools to protect and grow your financial future. Now, I want to summarize the essential ideas you should take with you so you can apply them with purpose and direction.

Final Thoughts

- Gold and crypto serve different roles in a portfolio, and both can be useful when you understand their strengths.
- Gold offers stability, history, and long term preservation, while digital gold offers innovation, portability, and growth potential.
- Both assets require responsibility, whether through physical storage or digital security.

- Diversification, patience, and thoughtful planning are key to building a strong strategy.
- Avoid myths, hype, and rushed decisions by focusing on research and long term goals.
- Understanding your risk tolerance helps you decide how to balance safety and growth.
- Trends, technology, and global behavior will continue shaping the future of both assets.

What You Should Take Away

As you look back on what you learned, remember that there is no single perfect asset or one size fits all strategy. Investing is a personal journey that depends on your goals, your comfort level, and the world you live in. Real gold and digital gold are powerful tools, but they are most effective when you use them with knowledge and intention. When you stay informed, stay patient, and stay focused on your long term vision, you put yourself in a strong position to succeed.

Simple Steps to Move Forward

- Start small so you can learn without feeling overwhelmed.
- Choose trusted dealers, platforms, and security tools.

- Build a simple, realistic portfolio plan that fits your goals.
- Review your strategy regularly and adjust when necessary.
- Keep learning as markets and technology evolve.

Last Thoughts

As you step forward, I hope you carry the confidence that comes from understanding both real gold and digital gold in a clear and practical way. These assets represent two sides of the modern financial landscape, giving you the chance to combine historical wisdom with technological innovation.

With the insights from this book, you can make decisions that support your stability, your growth, and your long term financial security. You now have the knowledge to move forward with a balanced and informed perspective, and I am glad I could guide you through this important journey.

About the Author

Roggie "Raj" Clark is an entrepreneur and a 10-year marketing professional with a proven track record in e-commerce and digital business growth. Having built and managed successful online stores with thousands of sales and consulted for numerous marketing clients, Roggie has mastered the intricacies of online marketing, branding, and consumer behavior. He has also written several popular books on digital marketing, SEO (search engine optimization), and programming (HTML, CSS, and JavaScript).

As a former marketing manager at a fintech company—a role he secured through his own marketing and financial expertise—Roggie gained firsthand experience in financial strategy and wealth-building. This journey inspired him to share insights with amateur investors, helping them save money, make smarter financial decisions, and build long-term wealth. Raj currently lives in Maryland with his sister and niece.

www.ingramcontent.com/pod-product-compliance
Lightning Source LLC
LaVergne TN
LVHW022314200926
848481LV00004B/1341

* 9 7 9 8 2 9 5 5 4 6 3 1 0 *